GW01465829

Jo

A survivor of human trafficking

by
Jean Olwen Maynard

*All booklets are published thanks to the
generous support of the members of the
Catholic Truth Society*

CATHOLIC TRUTH SOCIETY
PUBLISHERS TO THE HOLY SEE

Contents

ISBN 978 1 78469 025 0

What is human trafficking?

Slavery is supposed to have been abolished, but it's come back. Today we call it trafficking, and it's alive and well and thriving in the 21st century. Traffickers prey on the poor and powerless, using force or deception to abduct and imprison them, or otherwise establish control over them and deprive them of any freedom of action. Often the victims are removed to distant places, far from any family members or social networks that could protect them, and it is common practice to smuggle them across national borders. Huge profits are generated for organised crime by exploiting and selling the sexual services, labour and organs of trafficked human beings.

Trafficking wrecks the lives of millions of women and men, girls and boys across the world today. In 2013 a group of religious women met with Pope Francis to ask him to establish a worldwide day of prayer for victims of human trafficking. When he asked them what date they thought would be most suitable, they proposed the feastday of St Josephine Bakhita: 8th February, and so it was agreed. Herself a trafficked child who not only survived to tell her story, but went on to find inner healing and true happiness, Josephine Bakhita brings home to us the horror of trafficking, yet also offers a message of hope to its victims.

Black Mother

Children arriving for the first time at the Canossian Convent in Schio - to be enrolled in the day school or nursery, or the boarding unit, or just to take part in a sewing class or a youth club - were usually startled to find that one of the nuns was black. This was in the 1920s and 1930s and hardly anyone in this quiet little north Italian town had ever seen a black person before. Very small children had been known to run away screaming in terror. But the kindly African Sister never seemed embarrassed, and soon put them at their ease. All of them quickly grew to love her, and whenever she appeared they flocked to her side. It was customary to address the nuns as "Mother", and properly-speaking she should have been Mother Josephine. But everyone called her "Black Mother".

Every Sunday the children besieged her, clinging to her long skirts and clamouring for a story. Black Mother's stories left behind the same deep-down, satisfying feel as a good fairy tale. The fact that they didn't have any fairies in, and had happened "for real", was completely beside the point. Fairy tales come in all shapes and sizes, but essentially they offer assurances about life. A typical scenario has a young person leaving home, sometimes very abruptly, to go out into the big wide world, and there face a series of apparently insuperable obstacles. But the obstacles can be overcome, and overcoming them wins the reward of a kingdom and an ideal marriage and being "happy ever after". The underlying message is: "Don't be afraid, because a kind providence is watching over you, and - you'll see - everything will work out in the end."

Out of Africa

"My family lived in the middle of Africa…" Black Mother knew precisely where she was born: a village called Al-Qoz in Darfur. Its name meant "Sandy Hill", and it stood at the southern edge of the Sahara Desert in an area of rolling countryside known as Daju, almost exactly halfway between the continent's eastern coastline on the Red Sea and its western coastline on the Atlantic. She couldn't give the date of her birth, but it was guessed to be 1869. Her father was a landowner with a large staff of field labourers and herdsmen, and the village head man was her uncle. Clearly her family was economically well-off, but more importantly it was close and loving: "It was made up of father, mother, three brothers and three sisters, plus four others whom I never knew because they died before I was born. I had a twin sister; I've no idea what became of her, or of any of them, after I was stolen. I was as happy as could be, and didn't know the meaning of sorrow."

Darfur was destined to become part of Sudan, one of the largest countries in Africa, covering 728,215 sq miles. But until the end of the nineteenth century this area was not, and never had been, a cultural or political unit. In 1869 Darfur was still a small, independent sultanate, dominated by a tribe called the Fur from their strongholds in the high mountains of Jabal Marra to the north. The Fur had long been Muslim, but their subject peoples did not necessarily share their religious allegiance: the inhabitants of Al-Qoz, at that date, were not Muslims. In her reminiscences, Black Mother said nothing of structured religious observances. She did speak very vividly, however, of her own awakening spiritual awareness in response to the world around her: "Seeing the sun, the moon and the stars, the beauties of nature, I asked myself, 'Who is the owner of all these beautiful things?' and I felt a great desire to see him, to know him and to pay him homage."

The little girl had no idea of the political developments, far to the north, which were about to impact on Darfur. Muhammad Ali, a soldier in the Ottoman army, seized power in Egypt and forced the Sultan of Constantinople (modern Istanbul) to recognise him as governor. Neither he, nor any of the administrative and military leaders who rose to power with him, were Egyptian: they had all come from other parts of the Ottoman Empire to make their fortunes. Because the language they spoke among themselves was not Arabic but Turkish, they were generally referred to as "Turks", though often they were European Muslims: Muhammad Ali himself hailed from Macedonia. Once his position in Egypt was secure, he tried to expand into the Middle East, but was warned off by the European powers. So he turned his attention southwards up the Nile where, from 1820, he began carving out for himself a huge central African colony in the territory of Sudan.

Robber barons

In Sudan the Turks behaved like robber barons, unashamedly out to plunder the country for all it was worth, for the personal enrichment of themselves and Muhammad Ali. They had hoped to find gold, but there wasn't much there: the main form of wealth was slaves. Muslim Sudanese could not legitimately be enslaved themselves, but they were quickly forced to hand over a large proportion of the slaves who constituted their household retinues and labour force. The only way to reimburse themselves, and continue to meet the Turks' insatiable demands, was to seize increasing numbers of fresh slaves from among the "unbelievers" further south.

Muhammad Ali's successors, who ruled as hereditary governors of Egypt enjoying the title "khedive", were eager to adopt new technological and educational ideas from Europe and, together with the rest of the ruling class, became increasingly westernised in their outlook. Meanwhile the subjugation of Sudan continued but, as the western nations successively repudiated slavery, its continued prevalence in their dominions became an acute embarrassment to the khedives. Measures were launched to develop the Sudan economically, partly in the hope that the growth of "legitimate" trade would squeeze out slaving, and also to make it into a steady source of wealth to pay for Egypt's modernisation programme. Better agricultural techniques and new crops were introduced, and traders ventured up the Nile in search of ivory. Another eagerly sought-after product was gum-arabic, an exudate of the acacia senegal tree, used since ancient times as a food additive and in pharmaceuticals. Nevertheless, alongside all this "legitimate" economic activity, the slave trade continued to flourish.

African slavery took many forms, some of them relatively benign. Slaves in traditional societies were not necessarily ill-treated, and might live as subordinate members of extended households in conditions which compared very favourably with those of factory workers in nineteenth century Britain. But whenever slaving was driven by strong outside forces it necessarily entailed tremendous suffering, due to the violent measures used to obtain captives, and the brutality with which they were conveyed over long distances to the place of sale. Under pressure from international public opinion, the khedives began introducing anti-slavery measures, but these proved ineffectual. Because the Sudan was so vast, raiders and traders could usually evade police patrols.

Khedive Ismail, who succeeded in 1863, was determined to confer on his dominions the full benefits of western civilisation and, having come to the conclusion that his fellow-Turks were too inefficient and corrupt to accomplish the task, resolved to employ as his agents European Christians. During the ceremonies for the opening of the Suez Canal in 1869, which were graced by the presence of a glittering line-up of eminent Europeans, he successfully recruited the British explorer Sir Samuel Baker. Baker's mandate was to consolidate Egyptian rule over the whole of the Nile basin, and suppress the slave trade. He and his successor, fellow-Briton Charles George Gordon, greatly expanded Ismail's Sudanese empire, but completely failed to eradicate slaving. They merely rearranged it, driving the slavers away from the Nile to the overland routes through western Sudan.

In 1874, shortly after Gordon's arrival, Sultan Ibrahim Muhammad of Darfur was defeated and killed in battle by the notorious slave trader Zubayr. Darfur was absorbed as a Sudanese province, and from then on slavers from other parts of Sudan were free to raid into it.

Raiders

The Daju Hills would have been arid and bare but for the many streams flowing down from Jabal Marra. Fertile patches spread out on either side of the streams, and so Al-Qoz was surrounded by beautiful greenery. In Black Mother's story, the occasion on which she first learned the meaning of sorrow began with a happy outing in this lush countryside. "One day my mother decided to go out into the country where we had many fields full of crops, and herds of cattle, to see if all the workmen were attending to their tasks. She wanted all us children to go with her. But the eldest girl, who wasn't feeling well, asked if she could stay at home with our little sister, and Mummy agreed. While we were out in the fields we heard a great commotion: lots of shouting, and people running to and fro. Everyone immediately guessed what it must be - slavers raiding the village."

Rushing back home, they found the little sister - Black Mother's twin - shaking all over with terror. She'd managed to hide behind a broken-down wall, so the raiders hadn't found her, but the older girl had been taken. "I still remember how Mummy cried, and how we all cried. That evening, my father came home from work and heard what had happened. He flew into a rage, and immediately set out with his men to search all around, but in vain: we never heard anything of our poor sister ever again. That was my first sorrow and oh, how many, many more lay in store for me after that.

"One morning when I was about nine years old I set off after breakfast with one of my friends, who was twelve or thirteen, for a walk in our fields a little way away from home. After playing for a while we broke off, and became absorbed in gathering herbs. All of a sudden two ugly armed strangers emerged from a hedge. Coming up to us, one of them said to my friend: 'Let this little girl go over there to that wood to fetch a package for me. She'll come back straightaway. Carry on walking and she'll rejoin you in a minute.' Their plan was to get my friend out of the way, because if she'd been there when I was captured she'd have given the alarm." Although when telling the story years later, Black Mother thought she had been nine at the time, it is more likely that she was only seven. "I didn't suspect a thing. I went to do as I was told, just as I did for my Mummy."

"Hardly had I gone into the wood to look for the package, which I couldn't find, than I saw those two coming up behind me. One of them grabbed me roughly with one hand; with the other he drew a big knife out from his belt, pointed it at my side, and snapped: 'If you shout, you're dead! Move! Come with us.' The other man pushed me forward, digging the barrel of a gun into my back. I was petrified with fear, my eyes staring, trembling from head to foot. I tried to scream, but there was a lump in my throat: I couldn't speak or cry out. Brutally driven into the thick of the wood, by hidden paths, across fields, they kept me going at a forced pace till evening. I was tired to death. My feet and legs were bleeding, because of the sharp stones and the prickles of the thorn bushes. I was sobbing my heart out, but their hard hearts felt no pity."

A new name

Dusk was falling as the three emerged from the far side of the forest. Still they didn't stop, but the man holding the child suddenly paused and asked her what was her

name. She tried to answer but her voice wouldn't come out
properly. The other man snapped, "Call her Bakhita and
don't waste any more time on that snotty kid." He shook
his whip in her face: "Understand? From now on your
name is Bakhita. Don't forget it!"

It meant "Lucky", and as such it was a very common
name for slaves, because owners liked their slaves to bear
auspicious names. Similarly, in the time of the Roman
Empire, slaves were given names like Felix and Felicity.
One of the most revered early Christian martyr-saints was
Felicity, a slavewoman of Carthage in Africa.

"At last we took a break to get our breath back, in
one of the fields full of watermelons which grew in great
abundance in the countryside through which we were
passing. The men picked some fruit and gave me a piece
to eat, but I could hardly swallow it, even though I'd had
nothing to eat since morning. I couldn't do anything expect
think about my family. Heartbroken beyond all words, I
kept calling out for my Mummy and Daddy, but they
couldn't hear me. In any case the men made terrible threats
to shut me up and, tired and hungry as I was, forced me to
my feet again. The journey went on all night. At first light
we entered their village. I couldn't possibly have gone any
further. One of them grabbed me by the hand, dragged me
into his house and thrust me into a poky storeroom, full of
tools and broken bits and pieces. There weren't even any
sacks to lie on, or anything I could use as a bed: nothing

but the bare ground. He gave me a piece of black bread and said, 'Stay here'. Going out, he locked the door with a key.

"I was there for over a month. A small opening high up above was my window. The door was opened briefly from time to time to give me scraps of food. How I suffered in that place I can't put into words. I still remember all those terrible hours during which I exhausted myself with crying, eventually collapsing on the ground in a light swoon. Then my imagination took me among my own dear ones far, far away: I saw my beloved parents, brothers and sisters, and embraced them all with joy and tenderness, telling them how I'd been kidnapped and how much I'd suffered. At other times I imagined myself playing with my friends in our fields and felt happy. But woe is me, whenever I came back to the harsh reality of that horrid loneliness, a sense of despair came over me which seemed as if it would break my heart.

"One morning the door was opened earlier than usual. The master presented me to a slave merchant, who bought me and put me together with some other slaves of his. There were three men and three women, and a girl not much older than me. At once we set off. Seeing the countryside, the sky, water, being able to breathe free air gave me back a bit of life, even though I didn't know where we were going to end up. The journey lasted eight days nonstop. Always on foot through woods, over hills, through valleys and desert places. I'll describe how the caravan was organised. The men went in front and after them the women, linked together by great chains padlocked round their necks, either into pairs or into groups of three. If anyone turned or stopped, heaven help his poor neck and that of his companion! You could see round each person's neck big, deep sores that made you feel so sorry for them. As we went through village after village the caravan kept getting bigger. The stronger men were made to carry great loads on their shoulders for mile after mile, poor things, as if they were pack animals. We children weren't chained; we walked near the back, in the midst of the masters. The caravan only stopped a few hours to rest and eat, and at those times the chains were taken off the slaves' necks and put round their feet, a pace apart from each other, to prevent escape. They did that with us children too, but only at night.

"At last we stopped at the slave market. We were all put into a large room to await our turn for sale. The first to be sold were the most weak and sickly, for fear they would get worse and nothing could be had for them at all - poor victims! We two children - the girl who was about my own age, and me - found ourselves always together, because our feet were fastened together by the same chain. Whenever nobody was listening, we used to talk to each other about how we were stolen. We spoke of our dear ones, and the longing kept welling up inside us to return to our families. We wept over our unhappy fate - but at the same time, we were putting together a plan for flight. The good God, who watched over us without us even knowing it, gave us the chance: this is how it happened.

Escape

"The master had put us in a separate room and always shut us in, especially when he had to leave the house. It was nearly suppertime when he came back from the market leading a mule laden with maize. He took our chain off, ordered us to husk the corn-cobs and feed some of them to the mule, and absent-mindedly went away without closing the door. We were alone without the chain. In the providence of God, this was our moment!

"We looked at each other, linked hands, looked around and saw nobody, then were off into the open countryside, with no idea where we were going but with all the speed our poor little legs could give us. All night long we ran and ran, driven on by terror, in and out of the woods and through the desert places. Gasping for breath, we could hear in the darkness the roaring of wild beasts. Whenever they came close we climbed up into the trees for safety. One time we had just got down from our refuge, and carried on running, when we heard the typical hum of an approaching caravan. We hid behind some bushes bristling with thorns. For a good two hours one group after another passed just in front of us, but nobody saw us. It was the good God who protected us, nobody else."

Lost in the pitch dark forest, surrounded by perils worse even than brutal and greedy human beings, Bakhita suddenly saw a beautiful form appear in the night sky above, bathed in light and smiling down at her, pointing which way they should go. Without any explanation to her companion, who obviously saw nothing, she led them both in the direction indicated until, as dawn approached, the apparition vanished. This experience touched Bakhita very deeply, so much so that she could almost never bring herself to speak of it. Years later, however simply and openly she told her story to those who asked, whenever she got to this point she automatically left out the shining figure: she only ever mentioned it very privately, to a few people. At the time she'd been unable to make any sense of the experience, but now she knew it had been a vision of her guardian angel. The angel had guided her out of the forest and towards the right path: the path chosen lovingly by God for her to walk along - though, as she was to discover, it did not lead back to the home she had left.

"I made myself believe that once I'd got through the dangers I would quickly find my dear ones. This hope made me willing to suffer everything, and kept up my spirits. Alas, far from drawing nearer to them I was running I don't know how much further away... Towards dawn we stopped and took breath. How tired we were! Our hearts were hammering inside our chests, great drops of sweat trickled from every pore, a ravening hunger tore at our stomachs: we had nothing to eat. The longing to see our families again, and the fear of being caught, gave us strength to continue running, though not like before. But where would we end up?

"Towards sunset we saw a cabin. Our hearts leaped and we strained our eyes to see if it was our house. It wasn't - imagine our bitter disappointment! As we stood there thinking what to do next, a man appeared in front of us. Frightened, we made to run, but blocking the path he asked us, in a nice sort of way, 'Where are you going?' We remained silent. 'Come on,' he said, 'where are you going?'

"'To our parents.' 'And where are your parents?' 'There.' we replied, pointing confusedly without knowing where. Then he realised we were fugitives. 'OK', he said. 'Come and rest a bit. Then I'll take you to your parents.'

"Believing what he said, we followed him into the cabin. As soon as we entered we collapsed on the ground, completely done in. He gave us some water to drink, but we were so far gone we could hardly swallow. Then he left us alone and in peace, and we slept for about an hour before he woke us up, took us to his house, gave us food and water, and then put us into a big sheepfold full of sheep and goats. He made space to put down an *angareb* (string bed) and then, fastening us together by the feet with a heavy chain, told us to stay there in the sheepfold until further notice.

Slaves again

"That was that - we were slaves again. So much for taking us to our parents. We cried and cried. He left us there among the sheep and lambs for several days until a slave merchant passed, then took us out of the sheepfold and sold us to him. We had to walk a long way before rejoining the caravan. Imagine our surprise when we saw, among the slaves, some who had belonged to the master we'd escaped from. They told us how furious he'd been, and what a hue and cry there was when we weren't found. He was blaming and hitting out at everyone he met, and threatening to cut us into pieces if he found us. Now I understand more and more the goodness of the Lord who saved me then so miraculously." The rage of their previous owner isn't surprising, since Bakhita and her friend were the pick of his stock. Children between the ages of about ten and fifteen fetched the highest prices: he'd been hoping for far better profits on them than on the adult captives. Girls were at least as valuable as boys in Sudanese slave markets, and in Egypt and Arabia were usually more in demand.

"We marched on for two and a half weeks, always with the same order as described before. During that journey I was touched to see one poor slave who was in so much pain he could no longer stand. He begged to be allowed to sit and rest for a while, but the master refused to believe him, and hit him as if he was an animal. I saw him fall to the ground wailing, 'I can feel myself dying, I can't go on.' But that monster only beat him all the more, to make him get up. However, seeing that he really couldn't move, he had no choice but to take off the chain that linked him to his companion. The poor man moaned and pleaded for mercy but the master, filled with rage, ordered us to keep going while he stayed with that wretched slave. What did he do to him? Nobody ever saw him again.

"Arriving at last in the city, we were taken to the house of the Arab chief." Since she was kidnapped Bakhita had been forced to cover on foot almost 600 miles - not counting the escape attempt. The city was El Obeid, provincial capital of Kordofan. Kordofan was - and still is - the world's biggest producer of gum-arabic, and El Obeid its principal market. At that time it was the wealthiest town in Sudan, with a higher population than any other settlement: over 100,000 people. In the household of the Arab chief Bakhita was initiated into her new existence, quickly becoming fluent in Arabic and forgetting her original language. "He was a very rich man who owned a large number of slaves, all in the flower of youth. My companion and I were assigned, for the time being, as handmaids to the ladies and his daughters, who took a liking to us. It was the master's intention to make a present of us to his son on the occasion of his marriage. In that house we were treated well, and lacked for nothing. Only, one day I committed some fault in the eyes of the master's son. He immediately seized a whip to flog me. I fled into the other room to hide behind

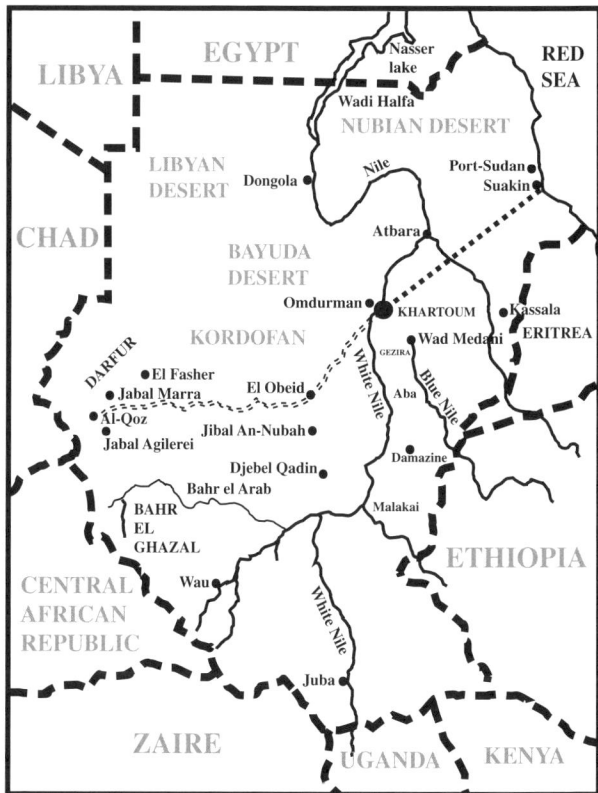

Map showing the Darfur region, and Bakhita's birthplace, Al-Qoz, in what is now Sudan. The double dashed line traces her journey as a trafficked captive; the single dashes, from Khartoum onwards, the journey she made willingly with Calisto Legnani.

his sisters. I should never have done that! He flew into a rage, dragged me out of there, flung me on the ground and with the whip and with his foot gave me so, so many blows. Finally, a kick to my left side made me lose consciousness. The slaves had to carry me to my sleeping mat, where I lay for over a month."

Another Bakhita

We have already said that Bakhita was very common as a slave-name. At this point in the story, let's take a look at another Bakhita who was living in El Obeid at this time. She had been born in Tongojo in the Nuba Mountains, kidnapped from there in 1854 when she was around twelve, and eventually sold in Egypt, but very soon after the original sale she was repurchased by a Catholic priest named Nicolò Olivieri. Her original name before she was captured by the slavers was Kwashe.

Fr Olivieri, then already in his sixties, had dedicated his life to ransoming slave children, and for that purpose set up extensive fundraising and support networks in Italy and Germany. After his death his work would be carried on by another Italian priest named Biagio Verri, and between them they must have rescued about 1,200 youngsters, arranging for them to be brought up and educated in Catholic orphanages and boarding schools in Europe. Mostly they ransomed girls, even though girl slaves cost more, because they were easier to place. Olivieri's work was praised by a number of influential Catholic leaders, including Don Bosco, but it also attracted sharp criticism. A very high proportion of the rescued children could not cope with the European climate, fell ill and died. The survivors, having completely lost touch with their roots, couldn't re-settle in Africa - but their institutional upbringing had isolated them from normal life in Europe too, so that they didn't seem to belong anywhere. A significant number resolved their dilemma by entering the religious congregations which had brought them up. Others fell in with plans laid for them by their educators that they should return to Africa as lay missionaries. These developments gave rise to further criticism, since their options appeared too limited for them to have made a truly free choice. Nevertheless, there were a few undoubted success stories - and Bakhita Kwashe was one of them.

Verona was a vibrantly Catholic city which had produced an impressive number of new initiatives to address the changing needs of the Church and the world. One was the Daughters of Charity, commonly known as Canossian Sisters after their foundress Maddalena di Canossa. Another was the Mazza Institute, which offered an excellent boarding school education, completely free of charge, to both boys and girls, and fostered a great many vocations to the priesthood and religious life. Its founder and director, Fr Nicola Mazza, agreed to give about fifty places to African girls. His intention was to train them as auxiliary missionaries, and encourage them eventually to return to Africa as assistants to some of his students, who were planning to go out as priests to Sudan. Bakhita Kwashe was among the first batch.

Vinco and Knoblecher

At a time when most parts of the African interior were so completely unknown, it had seemed a very good idea for pioneer missionary expeditions to aim for Sudan, ruled as it was by a government which enjoyed diplomatic relations with Europe. The first such expedition set out in 1847, made up of volunteers from several different countries under the leadership of Maximillian Ryllo, a Polish Jesuit with long experience in the Middle East. It succeeded in reaching Khartoum, the administrative capital of Sudan situated at the confluence of the White and Blue Niles. So far Khartoum was little more than a shanty town, and they set up their base in tents by the river bank. However the principle obstacle to European penetration into the heart of the continent remained the lack of immunity to its endemic diseases - particularly malaria. Very quickly Ryllo fell sick and died. Fr Angelo Vinco, an ex-student of the Mazza Institute, was ordered to return to Europe accompanying another sick missionary, leaving a Slovenian priest named Ignaz Knoblecher in charge. Despite the unpromising start, Vinco had fallen in love with Sudan. Suddenly reappearing at his old school, he inspired the director and many of the current students with his own enthusiasm. So it was that in January 1849 a seventeen-year-old philosophy student named Daniele Comboni knelt down before Fr Mazza, and vowed to devote his life to bringing the Gospel to central Africa.

Vinco meanwhile had made his way back to Sudan. He and Knoblecher then embarked on an historic journey up the White Nile to Gondokoro, where the Bari people lived. Before then, no white man had ever penetrated so far south. Vinco later journeyed south again, alone, and spent two years at Gondokoro, learning the Bari language and trying to present the Christian message to them in terms they could understand, until in January 1853 he fell ill and died. He was thirty-three.

After his ordination to the priesthood in 1854, Daniele Comboni returned to the Mazza Institute as a teacher to find Bakhita Kwashe in his class: she was probably the first African with whom he had ever come into direct contact. In 1857 he and some other ex-students set out for Sudan. On their way up the Nile they met a gaunt but venerable figure dressed in Arab robes: it was Knoblecher. He was heading north for Europe, planning to recuperate his health and regalvanise the mission's support networks, but - though not yet forty - he was in fact dying, and would never return to Africa. The Mazza priests took charge of a mission called Holy Cross which had been established among the Dinka people, but all of them soon came down with malaria and dysentery; after less than a year they were ordered to return to Europe. The Central African mission was reassigned to the Franciscan Order, which rapidly sent in fifty-two missionaries. Whereas previous expeditions had travelled slowly, taking frequent rests during which they could adjust to the climate, the Franciscans raced up the Nile as fast as possible. Within a few months over half were dead. Horrified, Rome ordered the mission abandoned.

Plan for the Regeneration of Africa

Nevertheless Comboni refused to give up. In September 1864, while praying for Africa at the tomb of St Peter during a visit to Rome, various ideas which had been tossing around in his mind came together. He set them down on paper as a Plan for the Regeneration of Africa, and quickly obtained appointments to discuss this Plan with the cardinals responsible for overseas mission, and with the Pope personally. It sought to build on previous experience, and learn from the mistakes that had been made. Mazza's vision of forming young Africans as evangelisers to their own people was retained, but some way must be found to educate them without taking them out of Africa. As for European missionaries, they must be enabled to acclimatise gradually before going into the interior, and never spend too long there without breaks to recuperate. Comboni's answer to both needs was to set up halfway houses on the "edges" of Africa.

He set up the first one in Cairo in 1867: a large campus with a church, residential accommodation, schools and workshops. To run the girls' school he brought in some Syrian, Arabic-speaking Sisters of St Joseph of the Apparition, and fifteen Europe-educated African girls of whom Bakhita Kwashe was one. In the same year, back home in Verona, he set up an institute to train further missionaries. He himself continued to travel around Europe, and backwards and forwards to Africa, consulting all sorts of experts, picking up ideas and consolidating contacts. Some people said he was crazy, others were impressed. The Bishop of Verona, Luigi di Canossa, admired his zeal and extended the necessary authorisation for his missionary endeavours. Since Comboni was having to spend quite a lot of time in Rome anyway, Canossa tasked him with helping to push forward the canonisation of his aunt Maddalena.

Missionary work required money. Comboni worked hard to reactivate Olivieri's support networks, and persuaded the Austrian Emperor, Franz-Josef, to confirm his continued patronage of those established by Knoblecher in central Europe. Imperial protection, as well as stimulating fundraising efforts, would secure for the mission the good offices of the Austrian consuls in Cairo and Khartoum.

The Verona Missionaries

In 1870 Comboni addressed an impassioned appeal for Africa to the First Vatican Council, gaining the support of the Pope and two hundred of the Council Fathers for the reopening of the mission. Later that same year the first four missionaries trained in his institute in Verona travelled out to Cairo, and began making exploratory tours into Sudan. Meanwhile Comboni also began training Sisters. The men and women who graduated from his institutes would eventually form a religious congregation: the Verona Missionaries.

At last, after years of careful planning and preparation, in 1873 Comboni returned to Khartoum, which was now an established city with 60,000 inhabitants. He reoccupied Knoblecher's mission centre there, as a base to handle communications and logistics, but quickly moved on to El Obeid to open what was to be his main mission: besides being a much healthier place to live than Khartoum, it was strategically better placed for access to the non-Muslim population of the Nuba Mountains. He used his good political connections with the khedival government to have slave raiding and trading in and around El Obeid declared illegal; however, like other such declarations, this proved a dead letter.

Whatever starry-eyed ideas might be entertained by anti-slavery campaigners in Europe, everyone on the ground in Africa knew that freeing slaves, once they had been brought thousands of miles across the continent, was highly problematic. Even if overwhelming military force could be deployed to overcome the objections of powerful slave-masters, the captives could not be returned to their original homes. Slavery in Sudan was so closely bound up with the whole social and economic system that "freed" slaves usually had no alternative way of making a living, so that their best option might be to stay with their owners. The Verona Missionaries recognised the impossibility of abolishing slavery overnight, but they were prepared to offer sanctuary to runaways who claimed to have been subjected to physical cruelty by their owners. The right of the missions to offer sanctuary was supposed to be upheld by the Austrian consul, but it was contrary to Egyptian law and extremely difficult to implement.

Comboni's missions always included schools. Muslim children were not supposed to attend them, but the traders resident in Sudanese cities included Copts from Egypt, and other Christians from the Middle East and Europe: their children provided the core intake. To them were added slave children, ransomed as and when funds were available. Among the pioneers of the El Obeid mission was Bakhita Kwashe, now an experienced teacher. The mission schools flourished, and she greatly enjoyed her work. When, a few years later, the first contingent of women missionaries trained by Comboni arrived in El Obeid, she got on so well with them that she decided to join their congregation, so becoming the very first African Verona Sister.

It is no disparagement of the love and courage shown by these early missionaries to recognise that any good they could do was only the tiniest, tiniest drop in the ocean. Out of El Obeid's 100,000 inhabitants, four in every five were slaves. Whatever success the missionaries had in rescuing a handful of individuals out of this vast number, the younger Bakhita whose story we are following was not one of the handful. She was completely unaware of the existence of the Christian mission, which as far as she was concerned might as well have been on another planet.

Passed from hand to hand

"When I had recovered from the thrashing, I was put to other work. But my destiny was marked: I was to leave that house at the earliest opportunity. The opportunity came three months later, and I was sold to a new master, a General in the Turkish army. He had his old mother and his wife living with him. Both of them were dreadfully cruel towards the poor slaves, who were kept constantly hard at work in the kitchen, laundry and fields. I and another young girl were put at the service of the two ladies. We couldn't leave them even for a moment: what with dressing them, fanning them and perfuming them, we never got a break. And woe betide us if accidentally, perhaps because we were so short of sleep, we hurt either of them the tiniest little bit: the lashes fell on our backs without mercy. In the whole three years I was in their service, I don't recall having got through a single day without a beating: no sooner did my wounds heal than more lashes rained down on my back - without my even knowing why.

"One day I was telling my companion how I ran away from my first master. The General's daughter heard everything and, for fear I might try to escape, she made me wear a great chain on my foot. I had to drag it round for over a month. It was only taken off on the occasion of a great Muslim feast, when they were supposed to release all the slaves from their shackles. Every day the slaves had to get up at dawn. The lady, the General's wife, was so zealous that sometimes she got up before everyone else, to keep watch in case anyone was even a minute late. Then she was after him with the whip, making him leap with pain. She never cared how late into the night the poor wretch might have had to toil the previous evening. The slaves all slept in a dormitory. We got nothing to eat until midday, when each of us was given a portion of meat stew, corn meal, bread and fruit. In the evening a scanty supper, and then to rest on the bare ground. Woe betide anyone who didn't keep absolute silence. Poor victims of human tyranny! Anyone who fell ill wasn't even looked at but just left there without treatment or help. Anyone who died was thrown into the fields or onto a rubbish tip.

"How much ill-treatment and whipping we poor slaves received, without any reason! For example, one day we found ourselves present by chance when the master had a row with his wife. To work off his bad temper he ordered us two to go down into the yard, and commanded two soldiers to fling us on the ground face up to be flogged. The soldiers set about the cruel torture with all their might, leaving both of us bathed in our own blood. I can still remember how the cane, aimed again and again at my thighs, was taking out skin and flesh, and gouged out a long narrow wound which pinned me down on my sleeping mat for months, unable to move. I had to bear everything in silence, because nobody came to dress our wounds or give us any word of comfort. Many of my companions in misfortune died under the blows they suffered."

Most of the children had heard the story many times before, but even those hearing it for the first time weren't upset or frightened. They knew this was a good story, a story with a happy ending. Everything came right eventually.

Tattooed

Black Mother had scars and marks all over her body. They were normally hidden under her enveloping habit, but the smaller children all knew about them and often begged her for a look. Although it embarrassed her to have to unbutton her clothes even a little way, she usually gave in and let them have a quick peep. If anyone asked about it, she just said, "Poor things, why not? Maybe it'll make them more grateful to Our Lord for letting them be born in Italy." To adults and older children, she would explain more fully about the marks.

"It was the custom for slaves, for the honour of their masters, to wear tattoos: designs or patterns cut into their bodies. Up to then I didn't have any, while my companions had lots, even on their faces and arms. Well, our mistress took a whim to make a 'present' of this sort of decoration to those of us who weren't already tattooed. There were three of us.

"A woman expert in this cruel art arrived. She took us to the porch, while the mistress stood behind us, whip in hand. The woman had a dish of white flour fetched, and another of salt, and a razor. She ordered the first one to lie down on the ground and two of the strongest slaves to hold her, one by the arms and the other by the legs. Then she bent over the poor girl and, using the flour, began to trace on her belly about sixty fine marks. I stood there, watching everything, knowing that afterwards they were going to perform the same torture on me. Once the marks were completed the woman took the razor and swish, swish, sliced along each mark she'd traced, while the poor girl groaned, and blood welled up from each cut. When this operation was finished she took the salt and rubbed it as hard as she could over each wound, so that it would go in and enlarge the cut, and keep the edges open. The agony and torment! The victim was writhing in pain, and I was shaking in anticipation.

"When the first girl was taken away to her sleeping mat, it was my turn. I didn't think I had the strength to move, but one glance at the mistress and her whip made me get down immediately onto the ground. The woman was ordered to spare my face, so she started off by making six designs on my chest and then about sixty on my belly, and forty-eight on the right arm. What it felt like I cannot put into words. I kept thinking, 'This is it; I'm going to die', especially when she rubbed the salt into me. Covered in blood, I was carried to my sleeping mat where I lay semi-conscious for hours on end. When I came to, I saw beside me the other two who, along with me, had been made to suffer this atrocity. For over a month all three of us were condemned to lie there, stretched out on the reed matting, unable to move, without even a piece of rag to dry the pus which seeped continuously from the wounds kept half open by the salt. I've still got the scars. I can honestly say the only reason I didn't die was through a miracle of the Lord, who destined me for better things." Black Mother was quite clear that the way she had been treated was very wrong. She hoped very much for the situation she had known in Sudan to be changed completely, so that no one else would have to suffer as she had. Nevertheless she didn't hate those who had inflicted so much pain on her, and wouldn't have them demonised. When one Sister exploded in righteous indignation against "those wicked slave-owners" she placed a finger on her lips: "Sshh… Poor things, they weren't wicked. They didn't know God. And also, maybe they didn't realise how much they were hurting me." On another occasion she smiled and said, "I pray for them a lot, that Our Lord who has been so very good and generous to me will be the same with them, and bring them all to conversion and salvation."

The Mahdi

Gordon's apparent success in suppressing slavery in Sudan had made good newspaper headlines in Europe, but he himself knew he was fighting a losing battle, and his efforts had infuriated many powerful groups. The fact that he was not only a foreigner, but also a Christian, could make it very easy to unite the different factions in an uprising against his authority. At the same time serious trouble was brewing in Egypt, where the country's modernisation along European lines had tied it very firmly into the global economy - an economy dominated by European capital. The Suez Canal had been built with Egyptian labour, but very soon the khedive was obliged to sell his shares in it to Britain, because his debts were spiralling out of control. In 1879 Ismail was deposed in favour of his son, Muhammad Tawfiq, who ruled thereafter as a British puppet. An attempt by indigenous Egyptians to resume control over their own country was ruthlessly suppressed. When Gordon heard what had happened he resigned, so creating an abrupt power vacuum in Sudan.

Times of extreme crisis throw up apocalyptic expectations. In some parts of the Islamic world, the expectation can focus on a mahdi, or divinely-appointed leader. On Aba Island, in the stretch of the White Nile which flows along the border of Kordofan, a pious young sufi named Muhammad Ahmad grew convinced that he was the longed-for mahdi, called by God to set right a world which had gone astray. On 29th June 1881 he proclaimed a new creed: "There is no God but God, and Muhammad is the Prophet of God, and Muhammad al-Mahdi is the successor of God's Prophet!"

Comboni, visiting his missions in Kordofan at the time, was aware of the nascent revolt but attached little importance to it: the new Governor-General, Ra'uf Pasha, had sent troops to put it down. Returning to Khartoum he reported sadly, in response to an enquiry from Ra'uf, that slaving continued to flourish in the Nuba Mountains. In October several of his missionaries fell ill, and he helped look after them before succumbing himself. On 10th October he died.

Successive armies were sent against the Mahdi, but each in turn was defeated. Bakhita and her fellow-slaves were told nothing about what was going on, but they were aware that their master was away from home; he must have been involved in some of the failed campaigns. Certainly he could see the writing on the wall and, around the middle of 1882, decided to get out of Africa before it was too late. "After an absence of several months, the General returned to Kordofan having made up his mind to return to Turkey. He set about making preparations for departure and, since he had a large number of slaves, he selected ten of them including me, and sold off the rest. We left Kordofan and after several days' journey on camelback we put up in an inn in Khartoum. There he put the word around to anyone who wanted to buy slaves.

Calisto Legnani

The Italian consular agent paid a call. I was told to bring him a coffee. I saw him examining me from head to foot, but never imagined he was planning to buy me. I only realised the next day, when the Turkish General told me to go with the consul's housekeeper to help her carry a package. This time I was really lucky, because the new master was so good and took a great liking to me. My job was to help the housekeeper with the domestic work."

The countries of western Europe all maintained representatives in Sudan, and those which couldn't afford a professional diplomat arranged for part-time cover by one of their nationals already there on business. Calisto Legnani, who had already spent two years trading in gum-arabic, was appointed consular agent in 1880. He must have made frequent trips to El Obeid, and been personally acquainted with the Turkish General from whom he purchased Bakhita. It's a fair indication of the failure of the many attempts to suppress slavery in Sudan that even resident Europeans routinely bought and held slaves.

Legnani was a frequent visitor to the Catholic mission in Khartoum. Did this mean he took Bakhita there, or at least mentioned it to her? No, it didn't. Even someone who took the Catholic faith seriously might have hesitated to try to share it with his Sudanese servants, who were automatically assumed to be Muslims. However, Legnani's visits to the mission did not indicate religious conviction. Every European in Khartoum visited the mission. The Italian traders attended Mass regularly, and were often pillars of the parish - even though in Europe they might never go inside a church, for they were all very gung-ho for Italy's recently-won unity and independence, and such an attitude at that date usually went a long with a sharp anti-Catholicism. In Khartoum there wasn't much else to do, and dropping in at the mission gave them an opportunity to meet fellow-countrymen, and helped assuage their nostalgia for Europe. In Khartoum as in El Obeid, Bakhita remained completely unaware that there was a Catholic mission in the town, and she had still never heard a word about Christianity. Nevertheless Legnani proved a decent and kindly master, and she was very happy in his service. "There were no scoldings, no punishments, no beatings! I couldn't believe I was enjoying so much peace and quiet."

In the camp of the Mahdi

For the missionaries in Kordofan, meanwhile, all peace and quiet was at an end: El Obeid was under siege by the Mahdists. The staff of an outlying mission at Dilling surrendered and were taken as prisoners to the Mahdi's camp, where repeated efforts were made to convert them to Islam. The Austrian consul in Khartoum sent money to ransom them, but it was refused. Eventually, on 27th September, they were told that unless they converted they would be put to death the following day. The eight missionaries - priests, Brothers and Sisters - spent the night praying and writing goodbye letters to their families.

At 9.00 am they were led out in front of the 40,000-strong Mahdist army, and ordered to kneel and bow their heads for the executioner's sword. Just then the Mahdi rode up on a white camel and ordered a stay of execution, to give them one more chance. Taken before the Mahdist leaders, each was asked, "Which do you choose: Islam or death?" Each one chose death. Most of the leaders argued that they should be killed, but Khalid Ahmad al Omarabi declared that Islamic law forbids the execution of churchpersons who surrender without fighting. The Mahdi acknowledged that he was correct. However the missionaries remained prisoners, and were not allowed to leave the camp.

In January 1883 El Obeid surrendered. Thirty horsemen came to the mission, and carried off Bakhita Kwashe together with four other Sisters. They too were ordered to become Muslims, but refused. They were made to march with the army, barefoot over the hot sand, sharp rocks and thorn bushes of the desert, and at one point a Sister was hung upside-down and beaten on the soles of her feet. To her relief, Bakhita Kwashe wasn't singled out to be treated any worse than the others, though as a Sudanese ex-slave she might have been considered technically an apostate from Islam. When the Mahdi heard how the nuns were being treated, he disapproved and ordered them brought into his own enclosure for safety. Later, some of the missionaries managed to escape and make their way to safety in Egypt; Bakhita Kwashe was one of those few.

The rest remained prisoners for many years, living in harsh conditions in which half of them died.

For the moment the revolt appeared confined to western Sudan, and Calisto Legnani saw no cause for alarm. He spent several months during the second half of 1883 travelling: first to Italy and then, in connection with his promotion to Vice-Consul, visiting the port of Suakin on the Red Sea, before settling back into his main residence in Khartoum. Gordon returned to the city in February 1884 with orders - if no agreement could be reached with the Mahdi - to evacuate it. Believing that a safe evacuation was impossible, he resolved instead to try to defend it. From September it was under siege by the Mahdists.

Even as the year drew to a close, most inhabitants remained confident that the British army was on its way, and all would be well. However, when Bakhita heard that Legnani was planning another trip to Italy she took notice - not because she was frightened, and anxious to get out of the beleaguered city, but for another reason that she couldn't clearly explain: "I don't know why, but when I heard him name 'Italy', although I knew nothing of its beauty and charm, a keen desire sprang up in my heart to accompany my master. He liked me so much I dared to ask him to take me to Italy with him. He explained to me how long and expensive the journey was, but I insisted so much that he agreed, to please me. It was God who wished it, I realised later. I can still feel the joy I experienced at that moment.

Mother Josephine praying in the convent in Schio, Italy.

We set off. By 'we' I mean the consul and his friend, a young black boy, and myself, riding on camels all together in a caravan. After a few days' journey we reached Suakin." Khartoum was by then virtually surrounded by rebel forces, but Legnagni and his friend, a fellow-businessman named Augusto Michieli, must have known a way for a small party to sneak through.

The fall of Khartoum

On the night of 25th January 1885, the Mahdi's forces crossed over the White Nile to mass around the southern ramparts of Khartoum, where a slight fall in the level of the river had exposed a sandbank. This foothold enabled them to breach the city's defences and, as the following day broke, take it by storm. Gordon was killed in the fighting, and many thousands of people - starting with the European residents and all identifiable Christians who refused to adopt Islam - were put to the sword. Bakhita's knowledge of the event was limited to what her owners chose to mention to her: "After about a month the consul and his friend received the sad news that a gang of rebels had entered the city of Khartoum, had destroyed everything, and taken possession of all the slaves. Since the consul and the other gentleman had been robbed of everything, they were very upset. If I had stayed there I would certainly have been stolen and what would have become of me? How much I thank the Lord for having saved me yet again! We stayed in Suakin for a month, then began our voyage by ship across the Red Sea and other seas as far as Genoa. There we took lodgings in a guesthouse whose proprietor was well-known to the consul's friend, and had asked him to purchase a black boy for him. So the boy who had been my companion during the voyage was immediately made over to him. The friend's wife had come to meet him and, seeing us two blacks, said she wanted one and asked her husband why he hadn't brought one for her and her little daughter. The consul, to please his friend and her, made a present of me to them." Legnani and the Michielis were all making for destinations in the Veneto region, on the opposite side of the Italian peninsula from Genoa. Probably they covered this last leg by train, but at a certain point the party broke up: "The consul headed for Padua, and I never heard anything more of him. My new master and mistress and I made our way to Mirano Veneto where, for three years, I was nurse to their little daughter."

Mirano is a small town a short distance inland from Venice, and the Michielis' family home stood in an outlying village named Zianigo. Bakhita's account, which was only written down years later, slides over a detail: Michieli's wife Maria Turina had a son of about five, and had given birth to a baby girl the previous summer - but this girl died very young and Bakhita never mentions her. The daughter she did look after was not born until February 1886.

Magnificently named Alice Alessandrina Augusta, she was known to Bakhita by her pet-name Mimmina. "The baby came to love me dearly, and I naturally came to feel a similar affection for her."

Shortly after Mimmina's birth Augusto Michieli returned to open a hotel in Suakin. The Red Sea port still remained in Egyptian hands: whether because Britain was prepared to defend it more effectively than Khartoum, or perhaps because the Mahdists were never all that interested in taking it so long as they could control its hinterland, it never fell to the insurgents. Bakhita, together with the rest of the Michieli family, remained in Zianigo; only at the end of 1886 did Augusto send for them all to come out and join him. During their absence the empty house, with the small farm attached to it, would be left in the hands of the Michieli's local agent Illuminato Checchini.

Farewell to Africa

"After three years had gone by I returned with the mistress to Suakin in Africa, where her husband was running a large hotel. We stayed for around nine months, after which the master decided that the whole family should make their permanent home there. However the mistress would have to return to Italy to sell off the property and pack up the furniture. I was supposed to stay meanwhile at the hotel with the baby, but my mistress didn't fancy travelling on her own, so it was agreed that we should both go with her. Then I bade in my heart an eternal farewell to Africa. An inner voice told me I would never see it again."

The return to Zianigo took place in the autumn of 1887. Maria Turina duly set about selling the house and land - naturally taking advice from Checchini. The agent's visits to the house led to some friction, as he was shocked to realise that Bakhita had never been offered religious instruction. He persuaded the Michielis' housekeeper to say prayers with the African girl each morning. It's unlikely that the housekeeper's devotions, whether rattled off in Italian or in Latin, meant anything to Bakhita, but the arrangement certainly annoyed their mistress. If Augusto was fundamentally irreligious, Maria Turina was more so. She wasn't Italian but Russian, daughter of a wealthy St Petersburg family and, although nominally Orthodox, like many upper-class Russians of the time she claimed to be an atheist. She didn't want Checchini, as she saw it, "upsetting the servants".

The Michielis belonged to that well-heeled class for whom Italian reunification and independence had brought solid benefits. By contrast Checchini, son of a village cart- maker, was essentially a peasant. He knew only too well that in the new Italy, conditions for the rural poor had deteriorated - and it was a matter of deep concern for him even though he, personally, was not too badly affected. He viewed his employers' fashionable superficiality about spiritual values with instinctive scepticism, and quietly set about subverting it. Although he'd never had much formal education, having left school early to help his father in the workshop, he had plenty of native intelligence and a mind of his own. He was deeply religious, and in his home parish of Salzano used to play the organ in church. He got on specially well with the parish priest assigned to Salzano in 1867, Fr Giuseppe Sarto, a remarkable priest unreservedly dedicated to his pastoral and charitable work; he and Checchini used to play cards together. They kept in touch even after Checchini's marriage in 1870, when he moved to Zianigo to make a career as a middleman and business agent for the local farmers and small landlords. He was well-known locally as a source of excellent advice, which was free for those in trouble, and he was very active in promoting self-help schemes such as savings banks and mutual assurance societies.

It took Maria Turina a whole year to sell off the property, and even then there were still some bits of business which couldn't yet be finished. She was missing her husband, so she decided to take a break, travel out to Africa and spend some time with him. Since she wouldn't be there long, it hardly seemed worthwhile to drag the baby out with her. She laid her plans before Checchini: could he suggest somewhere suitable for Bakhita and Mimmina to stay during her absence - preferably a boarding school where Bakhita could receive some education? (What she had in mind by education, and whether it was realistic given that Bakhita was nearly twenty and had never previously had any schooling, is not clear.) Checchini knew just the place: the Catechumenate in Venice. It was run by the Canossian Sisters, the same congregation which had a house in Mirano. Maria Turina must know how eminently respectable they were: they could certainly be trusted to ensure the two girls were properly looked after.

Catechumenate

Since Vatican II the term "catechumenate" has made a comeback: many Catholics today would recognise it as a process of Christian initiation. Probably to Maria Turina, however, the term meant nothing and - although her husband was a scion of the Venetian patriciate - she herself was unlikely to have known the history of the Catechumenate. It had been set up in 1557 purposely to house adult non-Christians wishing to receive instruction in the faith. Because such individuals were often rejected by their communities of origin and faced the loss of home, family and livelihood, the institution offered them shelter, and practical help in beginning a whole new way of life. Venice's widespread trading contacts and comparative religious toleration made it a meeting point of cultures, and the flow of converts remained impressive for well over a century.

Although the Catechumenate never achieved the security of lavish endowments, it enjoyed a certain social cachet which attracted interest and donations from the patriciate and, after beginning operations in rented premises, moved to a permanent site on the edge of the city. Twice the premises were rebuilt, each time on a larger and grander scale: there were separate sections for men and women, with a small church dedicated to St John the Baptist standing between. But after Napoleon crushed the independence of the Venetian Republic, the magnificent buildings fell into disuse. The Canossian Sisters had been asked to take over the women's section in 1848. They did run a school on the premises, though it was actually a day school for poor girls from the neighbourhood. They also maintained the historic links of the institution with the city's aristocracy, by organising prayer meetings and conferences for society ladies. Strictly speaking, they had no boarding school facilities. But naturally, if ever the opportunity arose, they would be more than happy to fulfil the Catechumenate's original purpose by offering religious instruction to prospective converts.

Checchini took it upon himself to negotiate the arrangements. Once he had explained the situation, the Sisters readily agreed to take Bakhita, but there was a technical difficulty about Mimmina. If she'd been unbaptised they would happily have stretched a point and put her down, as they planned to do with Bakhita, as a candidate for instruction, though she was not yet three. But the Michielis' irreligion was purely conventional and their children were all baptised. Maria Turina would not agree to separate arrangements being made for the two girls: they must be kept together. She expressed willingness to pay for their board and lodging, but since she was about to leave the country it might be difficult to hold her to this.

Resolving the difficulty took a whole month, during which Checchini visited the Michieli house frequently. One day he gave Bakhita a small silver crucifix. "Giving me the crucifix he kissed it with devotion, then explained to me that Jesus Christ, Son of God, died for us. I didn't know what it was, but impelled by a mysterious force I hid it in case my mistress took it off me. Before then I had never hidden anything, because I was never attached to anything. I remember how I used to look at it in secret, and feel inside myself something I couldn't explain."

"That is your home now"

Not until the very end of the year did Maria Turina, together with Illuminato Checchini, his wife and his five children, escort Bakhita and Mimmina to Venice and install them in the Catechumenate. To make sure his carefully laid strategy didn't fall through, Checchini had personally guaranteed to defray all expenses involved in looking after both the girls, if the Michielis defaulted. "When my mistress accompanied me to the institute, she turned round on the doorstep to bid me goodbye and said: 'There, that is your home now.' She said this without having any idea what she was really saying. Oh, if she had realised what was going to happen, she'd never have brought me there!"

Wide-eyed, Bakhita was led into the large, cool building and up a spiral staircase, above which the ceiling was painted to depict the Baptism of Christ. "I was entrusted, together with the baby, to a Sister who was well-experienced in instructing catechumens, Maria Fabbretti. Tears come to my eyes whenever I think of all the care she took of me. She asked if it was my desire to become a Christian and, hearing that I did desire it and was come with that intention, she was filled with joy. Then those holy Mothers instructed me with heroic patience, and brought me into a relationship with that God whom, ever since I was a child, I had felt in my heart without knowing who he was." Bakhita stressed the patience of Sister Fabbretti and her fellow Canossians because she knew it hadn't been easy for them. She was obedient and co-operative as ever, and eager to learn, but she could speak only a broken mixture of standard Italian and the Veneto dialect. It was very difficult for her to understand properly what was said to her, unless it related to practical matters immediately to hand. Everything had of course to be conveyed verbally, or through pictures; the instruction sessions could never be supplemented by giving her material to read later.

Not long after their arrival she and Mimmina were spotted from the balcony of a house just opposite by six-year-old Giulia Della Fonte, who began coming over each morning to play with the baby. Giulia was fascinated by the black nursemaid of whom Mimmina was clearly so fond. Bakhita was always smiling - and yet there was something odd about the smile: it was a kind smile, but it wasn't a happy one. Why was Bakhita so sad inside?

Unfortunately, there was no way of finding out: Giulia could hardly understand anything she said. Since the time she arrived at Legnani's house in Khartoum, Bakhita would have said she was happy. But deep inside, her spirit remained painfully crushed by her horrific experiences and, even though her circumstances had changed so dramatically, she couldn't just shrug off the memories. Nevertheless, the hope had begun to dawn in her that a healing of her spirit might be possible.

Bakhita soon realised that whether or not other people understood her, she could always talk to God who understood everything, and didn't even require words. When left to her own devices, even while keeping an eye on Mimmina, Bakhita made the most of her opportunities for prayer. She often spent time in front of the large crucifix in the downstairs parlour. There was also the domestic chapel, where a statue of Our Lady of La Salette had been installed making it into a minor pilgrimage centre, or St John the Baptist next door. Alternatively, with Mimmina skipping along beside her, she could take a little walk round to Our Lady of Health, a church whose dome she could see from the window of their room. In that church there was an old icon of the Madonna and Child brought from Crete by the evacuated garrison when the island, a Venetian colony since the Fourth Crusade, was surrendered to the Turks in 1670. As in so many of Europe's most venerated Marian images, the figures depicted in it were black.

"No"

The best part of a year went by as if in a lovely dream, until on 27th November 1889 Maria Turina turned up again. All her business had been settled, and it was time now for Mimmina and Bakhita to travel back with her out to Africa, this time for good; Bakhita's new job behind the hotel bar was waiting for her in Suakin. And it was then that Bakhita said no: she wasn't going. "I refused to go with her to Africa because I was not yet well-enough instructed to be baptised. I also thought that, even if I had been baptised, it wouldn't be easy to practise my new religion there, and therefore it was better for me to stay with the Sisters."

Never before in her life had Bakhita flatly refused to obey an order. Maria Turina went through the roof. She raged and stormed at Bakhita, reminding her of all the Michielis had done for her, pointing out all the arrangements that had been made on the assumption that she would continue to be part of their household, and threatening her with dire consequences if she was so silly as to upset everything.

In the nineteenth century it was generally assumed that, for any young woman, to dare to make her own life decisions was both wrong, and dangerously foolish: she must defer to her parents or, in the case of a servant with no family of her own, her employers. Behind this assumption lay a harsh reality: as with domestic slaves in African societies, the shelter even of an exploiting household was usually a far better option than any of the likely alternatives.

Bakhita didn't feel in the least indignant at Maria Turina's attitude; on the contrary, she saw it as largely justified. If the Michielis had been cruel masters the issue might have seemed more clear-cut, but they weren't; they really had tried to do what they thought was best for her. Also, she was emotionally attached to the family, and positively adored Mimmina. Every accusation went through her like a knife. Feeling horribly torn apart, again and again she was on the point of giving in. What stopped her was not the belief that she had the right to do what she wanted with her own life, but the recognition that she owed a higher loyalty to God.

Eventually Maria Turina stormed out. Exhausted, Bakhita went down to the parlour and spent a long time praying in front of the crucifix there. "It made me suffer to see her so disgusted with me, because I really liked her. It was Our Lord who gave me strength to be so firm about it, because he wanted to make me his. How good he is!" Her ordeal wasn't over. Next day Maria was back, together with a lady friend, someone clearly very rich and important. Together they resumed the attack, alternately pleading and threatening. Still Bakhita wouldn't give in, and after they'd gone she was back praying in front of the crucifix.

Patriarch and Procurator

By now everyone in the Catechumenate knew about the row, which was creating tremendous embarrassment. The Sisters, although they liked Bakhita and would have loved to keep her with them, tried to persuade her to do what Maria Turina wanted. But she insisted: "No. I won't leave the house of Our Lord. It would be the ruin of me." What could she mean by that? After being excluded from the rest of Sudan, the Verona Missionaries had established a mission in Suakin, so it wasn't a place without any Catholic presence or access to the sacraments. Moreover the Mahdist regime itself had been defeated and overthrown by Lord Kitchener the previous year, bringing Sudan under British rule. There seemed no obvious reason for Bakhita to be so dead set against returning to Africa. Why give up the prospect of a secure home and job for life, and alienate the wealthy family which had offered her their protection? For her to stay in the Catechumenate might be no problem for the next year or so, but what about her long-term future? However Bakhita instinctively knew that she would not be capable of living, in its fulness, the Christian life to which God was calling her in baptism, if trapped in the profoundly unsupportive environment of an irreligious household in a non-Christian country.

Behind all other considerations lay the basic question of Bakhita's legal status: did the Michielis legally own her? Fr Jacopo, the elderly aristocratic priest who was Rector of the Catechumenate, didn't know what to do. When Bakhita, despite everything, persisted in her refusal, he decided to seek advice from higher up and wrote to the Patriarch of Venice, Domenico Agostini. The Patriarch in turn sought an opinion from the Royal Procurator, who replied categorically that slavery did not exist in Italy: therefore Bakhita was free, and could not be compelled to return to Sudan. Maria Turina herself approached the Procurator, but got the same response.

On the third day, 29th November, a summit meeting was held in the parlour. Maria Turina arrived flanked by the lady friend who'd come before, and a male relative wearing the impressive uniform of an army officer. The Patriarch was there, the Priest-President and Mother General of the Canossian congregation, Fr Jacopo, and some of the Sisters who worked in the Catechumenate. The government authorities were represented by the Procurator and the Prefect. "The Patriarch spoke first. There followed a long discussion, which concluded in my favour. Mrs Turina, weeping with rage and disappointment, seized the child who didn't want to be separated from me, and was clinging to me to try to make me come. I was so upset I couldn't say a word. I left them weeping and went out, satisfied that I hadn't given in."

Next morning Giulia Della Fonte danced in as usual to find Bakhita sitting alone in floods of tears. Mimmina had gone away to Africa, and she would never see her again.

Baptism

Bakhita was baptised in the Church of St John the Baptist on 9th January 1890. Illuminato Checchini and his family were the first to arrive, and little Giulia was there with her mother and aunt. Besides this handful of personal contacts, the flower of the old Venetian nobility turned out for the occasion. At the request of his devout but bedridden wife, Countess Giuseppina, and perhaps also of his relative Fr Jacopo, Count Marco Avogrado di Soranzo stood godfather, and Lady Margherita Donati was godmother. Three baptismal names were conferred - Giuseppina Margherita Fortunata: Giuseppina (Josephine) for the Countess; Margherita (Margaret) for her godmother; and Fortunata as the Latin translation of Bakhita's Arabic name. Immediately after her baptism she was confirmed and given her First Communion by the Patriarch.

The ceremony over, those present were invited into the parlour for refreshments. Giulia, overawed, stood off to one side watching Bakhita being lionised by all the lords and ladies. Eventually Bakhita saw her, smiled and beckoned her over and kissed her, and then kept her close. Clearly she felt just as out of place as the child. Neither of them dared sample the refreshments. When everyone else had gone, Fr Jacopo kindly invited just the two of them to join him for lunch in his own quarters. Giulia was overwhelmed to see Bakhita's radiant joy: the sadness was gone, and she seemed completely transfigured. Thinking that this must be what a saint looked like, the little girl kissed Bakhita's hands again and again.

To know the Lord and to belong to him was something so wonderful that all the pain and sorrow of the past shrank into a speck of insignificance beside it. Even more wonderfully, Bakhita understood now that the Lord had always been there, caring for her and watching over her. If he had allowed the pain and sorrow, there must have been a purpose in it. To understand what that purpose could have been was beyond her, but that didn't matter; he knew, and she was content to trust him.

It was traditional for new converts to remain in the Catechumenate for a whole year following baptism, for their instruction to be consolidated. During this time Giulia continued to visit Bakhita and enjoy her company, attracted now not only by her natural goodness but by the happiness that shone out of her, a happiness that never seemed to evaporate. Checchini also kept in touch, and made it clear that as soon as she was ready to resume normal life, there was a place for her in his family. She would become an honorary daughter and, as such, would have a dowry settled on her so she could look forward to making a comfortable marriage: there need be no danger of becoming stuck in a religious institution with nowhere else to go . Nevertheless, at the end of her neophyte year Bakhita begged the Sisters to let her remain. They agreed, and she continued to live in there up to the summer of 1893.

"I stayed in the Catechumenate for four years, during which time I was hearing more and more clearly in the depths of my soul a gentle voice drawing me to want to become a Sister myself. In the end I spoke about it to my

Mother Josephine in the convent gardens, Schio, Italy.

confessor. He suggested that I should speak to the Superior, Sister Luigia Bottesella, who wrote to the Superior of the Mother House in Verona, Mother Anna Previtali. That good Mother not only agreed to my request, but added that she herself wished to have the satisfaction of clothing me in the holy habit and, in due course, to receive my profession."

In order to confirm her vocation by first "returning to the world", Bakhita now left the Catechumenate to spend three months with the Checchini family in Zianigo. She enjoyed this interlude of normal family life, but it didn't raise any doubts about the way of life towards which God was leading her. "On 7th December 1893 I entered the novitiate, right there in the House of Catechumens in Venice. After a year and a bit had gone by I was called to Verona for my clothing." Everything seemed to be going smoothly; neither she nor her superiors felt any doubts about her vocation. However at that time nobody was allowed to take religious vows without prior examination by someone fairly senior in the hierarchy, who was responsible for establishing that they had the personal maturity to make a free choice, and had not been improperly pressurised. In Bakhita's case, the examination was conducted personally by the Patriarch of Venice - now no longer Agostini, who had confirmed her, but Checchini's former parish priest Giuseppe Sarto. He told her: "Don't have any fears about taking your holy vows. Jesus wants you, Jesus loves you. And you are to love him and serve him always in the same way."

In the house of Our Lord

"I returned to Verona to pronounce my sacred vows on 8th December 1896. God allowed the ceremony to take place in time for Mother Previtali to see it, as she had so much wished to, since she was to pass away a month later on 11th January 1897. It gave me great satisfaction to be given the medallion of Our Lady of Sorrows by the Reverend Mother Superior, and be received into the community. It was the Feast of the Immaculate Conception 1896."

The Checchini family were present - of course; they would always remain her "family", and even after Illuminato himself died she would never lose touch with his children and grandchildren. After the ceremony there was a special visit to be made: the newly-professed Sister was escorted to the ancestral mansion of the Canossa family, to be given a guided tour of the foundress's childhood home, and meet the 87-year-old Bishop Luigi di Canossa who was most anxious to see this unusual new recruit to his aunt's congregation.

For another five to six years, Black Mother continued to live quietly in the familiar and beloved surroundings of the Catechumenate in Venice. Not having any particular area of responsibility assigned to her, she was no doubt called upon quite frequently to help out with the cooking and cleaning, and occasional supervision of small schoolgirls. But the activity which took up most of her time was handcrafting articles for sale on behalf of overseas missions. She did simple embroidery and handloom-weaving, and beadwork using the coloured glass beads cheaply mass-produced in nearby Murano. She particularly enjoyed the beadwork, and it became a hobby which she kept up throughout her life, turning out little items as gifts for friends who treasured them because of the love she put into making them. As well as fancy-work, she sometimes helped embroider vestments and altar cloths. By now she had acquired some basic literacy, though she only ever read her prayer book and the Canossian Rule - and perhaps also the Gospels, since she certainly came to know their stories very well.

In 1902, in compliance with the express wish of Patriarch Sarto, she was moved to the Canossian house in Schio. When told of the transfer she just smiled and said, "We're always in the house of Our Lord." The following year, to everyone's great surprise, Sarto had to leave Venice for ever when he was elected Pope; he took the name Pius X. Except for temporary transfers, Schio was to remain Black Mother's home for the rest of her life. The superior, Mother Margherita Bonotto, appointed her assistant cook, and in 1907 she was promoted to head cook. All the Sisters and children were delighted with the choice. It's never easy to cook for large numbers, but she saw it as a service of charity and did her utmost to produce really nice meals. She never minded putting in extra work to produce special menus for invalids, and she was careful to remember and keep food hot for Sisters whose work schedules prevented them coming at the main mealtime. In 1910, in obedience to her superior, she dictated an account of her life to be written down by one of the other Sisters.

Field hospital

When the First World War broke out Italy, though formally allied to Germany and Austria-Hungary, was under no obligation to get involved and at first remained neutral, but in May 1915 came in on the Allied side after being promised territorial gains at Austria's expense. The Italian government was particularly keen to annex South Tyrol, a largely Italian-speaking region which at that time still belonged to Austria. But the decision for war had been a gamble, taken in the belief that the Allies were on the brink of victory. Italy was desperately unprepared to fight, and the Austrian units rushing in to defend South Tyrol, which they considered an integral part of their own country, put up a tenacious resistance.

One night in May 1916 a column of wounded soldiers reached Schio from the front. An officer knocked on the door of the Canossian convent to ask if some space could be found for them, and very quickly the house was turned into a field hospital. Most of the Sisters were transferred to Mirano, but Black Mother stayed on, still as head cook though now with soldier-orderlies assigned to work under her in the kitchen. She also sometimes helped out with the nursing. There wasn't always enough bedding, and once when a man was brought in with a fractured skull, she ran to fetch her own pillow for him to lie on. The patients loved chatting to Black Mother, and the convalescents would all gather round to hear her tell her life story. She also talked to them, and to the orderlies, in no-nonsense terms about God; wouldn't tolerate bad language; and reminded them to go to confession. Not all of them appreciated the "preaching", and some of the orderlies decided to play a trick on her: when she was walking past they suddenly set off an ear-shattering alarm. She didn't turn a hair. Astonished, they asked, "Aren't you afraid of death?" "Anyone whose soul is in the right place doesn't have to be afraid," she answered.

The war continued to go badly for Italy. Morale was low among the poorly-equipped and abysmally-led armed forces, and among the civilian population faced with shortages of basic foodstuffs. Everyone was on edge. Once when Bakhita went out for a walk with her Mother Superior a military policeman tried to arrest her, assuming that any non-native was automatically a spy. In October 1917 the Italian line collapsed at Caporetto, allowing the Austrians to push forward for about a hundred miles to Monte Grappa, within sight of Schio. The disaster caused consternation throughout Italy. But a year later the disintegration of Austria-Hungary made it possible to launch a counter-offensive, allowing the Italian army to establish effective occupation of the contested territory before, on 3rd November 1918, hostilities formally came to an end.

A serious illness

In 1922 Bakhita fell ill. The doctor diagnosed pneumonia, and advised the Sisters to call a priest. But a few days after receiving the last rites she turned the corner and began to recover. When the doctor informed her she was off the danger list, he was taken aback to hear her say: "What a pity! When I was already so well on the way out, it would have been better to keep going. Now I'll have to do it all again." Following her illness Black Mother was relieved of her post as head cook, and given lighter work. For a number of years she served as portress, opening the door to the mothers bringing their children to school and nursery each morning, and dealing with contractors and deliverymen, and general callers. Lots of people used to make up excuses to drop in at the convent just out of curiosity to see the black nun. The odd thing was that, after they'd been talking to her for just a few minutes, they felt as though they'd known her all their lives, and were pouring out all their sorrows and worries. Because she'd known what it was to suffer, she always understood. But she wasn't just a sympathetic listener: from her they could draw strength and courage to face life again without fear.

In August 1927 she had the joy of taking her perpetual vows, in the Canossian house in Mirano. Early November 1930 found her temporarily at another of the congregation's Venice houses where, in obedience to the Superior General Maria Cipolla, she underwent a series of interviews in which she recounted her life story to Ida Zanolini to be written up for publication. This biography, "A Marvellous Story", sold like hot cakes in Italy at two lire a copy, and was also translated into other languages, and tourists began travelling to Schio wanting to meet its heroine. Called down to the parlour on one occasion at a particularly inconvenient moment during recreation, she quipped wryly: "Mother, if it costs two lire to read me, how much does it cost to see me?" Although she struggled hard to overcome her irritation, and always received even the most insensitive visitors with humble courtesy, she never viewed her meteoric rise to fame as anything other than an unmitigated nuisance.

On tour

Nevertheless, towards the end of 1932, her superiors resolved to put her celebrity status to practical use. She was asked to go on tour around the towns and villages of northern and central Italy, to participate in a series of publicity and fundraising events in support of the congregation's foreign missions. Although Black Mother could almost always establish rapport, and make herself understood well enough, in any face-to-face situation, she froze completely in front of a large audience - and in any case her Italian wasn't up to giving a formal speech - so she was teamed with another Sister. Leopoldina Benetti was likewise in her early sixties, but an experienced missionary who had spent thirty-five years in China. At each gathering Mother Benetti delivered a talk on the missions. She then recounted the "Marvellous Story", while its subject sat quietly beside her on the platform, and only at the end turned to her and asked her to say a few words. Immediately Black Mother hopped up and thanked everyone for coming, and then just said simply, "Be good. Love Our Lord." Sometimes she added, "Pray for those who don't yet know him. It's such a great grace to know God!" Then she sat down again.

Meanwhile Mussolini's Fascist dictatorship, which had promised great things to Italy, was signally failing to deliver. To bolster his credibility he needed to win a dazzling victory - anywhere, anyhow. The choice of target was easy: Italy had been smarting ever since the humiliating defeat in 1895 of its first attempt to invade Ethiopia. The time had come for revenge, and in October 1935 the second, successful invasion was launched. The campaign was over in six months. In December 1936 Black Mother, together with a group of young missionaries about to depart for Italy's new African colony, was formally received by Mussolini at the Palazzo Venezia. As yet, even well-informed circles in Europe did not know that, on his instructions, his army had ruthlessly massacred Ethiopian prisoners-of-war and wiped out whole villages with poison gas. Black Mother certainly could have had no idea at the time, and she may never have known. Nor do we have any record of what, if anything, she thought of the dictator. However it's probably safe to assume that she found more personal significance in a subsequent audience with Pope Pius XI.

These two receptions in Rome were the culmination of her mission promotion campaign. Much to her relief, the heavy programme which had been going on with hardly a break for about three years now came to an end. She had not enjoyed those three years at all. However unselfconscious she might be in Schio, she found it a heart-wrenching ordeal to be constantly on show in front of huge crowds of people whom she would never have time to get to know properly.

The presentations had been wildly popular. Very often, when they were held in a town, the traffic was snarled up in all directions with people trying to get there. Mother Benetti knew perfectly well that they weren't coming to hear her talk but to see Black Mother - and there was never any indication that they were disappointed with her when they saw her. But why all the excitement? Of course, her colour made her a curiosity, though she wasn't the only black Sudanese nun in north Italy; thanks to the ransoming efforts of Frs Olivieri and Verri, there were several others. In the course of her tours she had been taken to meet one of them: Sr Maria Agostina, a Visitation nun in an enclosed convent in Soresina. The Clarist Sr Maria Giuseppina (Zeinab Alif), originally from Kordofan, would have been a more obvious candi date for celebrity status: she was well-educated, showed outstanding leadership skills, and had served as abbess of her convent. Nevertheless it was Bakhita's story that really hooked people's imagination. A large part of the reason, certainly, was that she had undergone more dramatic physical sufferings than any of the others.

Straightforward curiosity about her colour had never upset Black Mother, even when expressed in particularly stupid ways. Once, on a train journey, a woman had started talking about her to Sr Benetti, asking how long she'd been in Italy. When told fifty years, she'd expressed amazement: "So it's taken fifty years for the palms of her hands to turn white." Black Mother broke in, "Give me another fifty years and the backs will turn white too."

However the "Marvellous Story" had evoked a huge upsurge of cheap sentimentality, and whenever Black Mother had to deal with people en masse, it was this element which she found most noticeable. It caused her agonies of distress. Mostly she refused to talk about her unhappiness except to God, but occasionally - when she could see that another Sister was deeply concerned and worried about her - she would try to explain. She didn't like the crowds and the way they pressed up against her, and she didn't like the fuss. But most of all she was upset by the way, after listening to her story, everyone felt so sorry for her and kept saying, "Poor thing, poor thing."

Why did they keep on and on missing the point? Why this total failure to understand that her story was a happy story, to grasp the Good News that God had given her the mission of proclaiming to the world? All her suffering had been for a purpose. It had been the way chosen by God, in all his great love and wisdom, to bring her by a sure and safe path into the kingdom of heaven, where she would live happily ever after, lost in adoration of the Divine Bridegroom. "I'm not a poor thing because I belong to the Master, and I'm in his house. People who don't know Our Lord - they're the ones who are poor!" With the children in Schio, she had never come up against anything like this. They had asked her directly and straightforwardly, and she had replied in the same way: "If I were to meet those who kidnapped me, or even those who tortured me, I would kneel down and kiss their hands. Because, if those things had not happened, I would not have become a Christian and would not be a Sister today."

Black Mother stayed on for another two years at the Canossian house in Vimercate, where the missionary novitiate was located. Occasionally she went off again with Mother Benetti in response to a request for speakers at a fundraising day, but most of the time she served as portress minding the entrance lodge. There, while the worst of the pressure was off, she could still play a key role in fostering mission work - which was certainly something she cared very strongly about. Most visitors to the house were parents of prospective missionaries, many of whom had still not come to terms with their daughters' choice. Black Mother would urge them to look at it from another point of view: "How many thousands of people in Africa would be brought to the faith, if only there were missionaries to tell them that God loves them, and that Jesus Christ died for them."

It was precisely for the sake of all those people in Africa that she had put up with the misery of being on tour. "Let's hope it'll help the missions, and especially my missions, and it doesn't matter to me that I'll never see them on this earth, because I'll see them in heaven." She knew very well that helping the missions wasn't confined to fundraising, or going out to Africa as a missionary; she was making the most effective contribution possible just by doing what she was asked to do, and offering up her sufferings to God in humble obedience. This insight enabled her to help a heartbroken novice who was being sent away from Vimercate because her health wasn't up to scratch: her dream of going to the missions was dashed for ever. Black Mother said, "Courage: you and I will both of us be saints and missionaries, and save many souls, by staying here."

"Schio will be spared"

At the end of 1938 Black Mother, now nearly 70, returned permanently to Schio. Partly due to age and arthritis, but also because of the long-term effect of the terrible injuries she had suffered when young, her health was deteriorating badly and she was finding it difficult to walk. Although she continued to help out with household chores around the convent, it was as and when she could: she would never again be charged with specific responsibilities. Following a fall in 1942, she needed a stick to get around, and by December 1943 when she celebrated her golden jubilee - fifty years as a Canossian Sister - she was using a wheelchair. One day a visiting bishop asked her what she was doing, just sitting there. She replied cheerfully, "I'm doing what you yourself are doing: the will of God."

Everyone was terrified when bombing raids began over Italy. Time and again came the question, from visitor after visitor, "Black Mother, will the planes bomb Schio?"

"No, don't worry. Schio will be spared." She insisted that no bombs would fall on any of the houses, and whenever the sirens sounded, and planes were seen flying overhead, she just sat in her room in her wheelchair, paying absolutely no attention. The other Sisters begged her to let them take her down to the air-raid shelter, but she refused. "No, no, Our Lord saved me from the lions and the panthers; do you think he can't save me from the bombs?"

People began saying to each other in the street that they didn't think the town would be bombed, because "in Schio we have Black Mother and she's a saint!" But on 14th February 1945 sixteen bombs fell on one wing of the Rossi textile mills, killing fourteen workers. Panic-stricken people ran to the convent: "Mother, don't you see they've dropped on Schio after all?"

"Certainly. And they'll drop again, but not on the houses. No private homes will be touched." And so it turned out. Bridges and military targets were bombed and strafed all around, and on one occasion fifty bombs dropped on the outskirts of the residential area but failed to explode. Not a single house was even damaged. Nevertheless, when Schio was liberated and the other Sisters were celebrating like everyone else, she issued a warning: "Pray, and be good - otherwise something worse will befall Schio." This prophecy also came true during the political infighting that broke out in this time of confusion. About a hundred local people accused of pro-Fascist activities (mostly quite minor) were locked up in the town gaol, and a group of armed Communist expartisans forced their way in and opened fire. Fifty-four detainees - including a number of women and teenagers - were killed in cold blood. Similar atrocities occurred in other parts of Italy around that time, but the massacre in Schio was by far the worst.

By this time Black Mother's health had deteriorated to the point that she was largely confined to bed. Being too ill to attend Mass didn't worry her, as she said her guardian angel would be present on her behalf. On one occasion a Sister got very upset to find that nobody had bothered to bring her Communion, but she said, "If he comes, that's fine, but if not, he's within me anyway and I am adoring him." The doctors compiled a long list of all the things that were wrong with her but, although she dutifully took all the medicines prescribed, they couldn't do a lot to ease her pain. Certainly she must have been suffering a great deal, but she only said, "As Our Lord wishes - it's up to him to decide." If she was uncomfortable at night she wouldn't call the Infirmarian: "Why should I disturb the sleep of those who need to sleep? I can rest later, but that Mother has work to do during the day. Anyway, if I suffer a bit it doesn't matter. I owe Our Lord so much that what I offer him is nothing."

"I'm going to heaven"

Towards the end of 1946 she took a turn for the worse and agreed to receive the Last Rites, though she knew she wasn't actually dying yet and said so. At 11.00 on the morning of 8th February 1947 a priest came to her room and jokingly asked, "How do you feel about receiving Communion now?" "I'd better, because afterwards there'll be no point…I'm going to heaven."

Towards evening she said, "The chains on my feet are so heavy." The Infirmarian thought her mind was wandering;

she pretended to be taking off the chains, while actually lifting away the bedcovers. Black Mother went on: "That's fine. Now I must go over there, to St Peter." "Yes, sure," replied the other Sister. "We'll go over to the cathedral straight away, arm in arm, and walk up the long stairs." "No, not that St Peter's there, but St Peter in heaven. I'll introduce myself to him and ask him to call the Madonna to me…" At that moment Black Mother's face was transformed with a radiant smile, as if she really was seeing the Madonna. "Look, look! You're here? Come, come, let's go to the foundress… So, when I'm there, I will never have to go away again, and I'll be there for ever." Those were her last words.

Next morning was Sunday, and Black Mother's death was announced in all the churches in Schio: if anyone wished to pay their respects, they should go to the convent where her body had been laid out in an open coffin. The first to come in was an unemployed workman. Approaching the coffin, he took off his cap and started not whispering a prayer, but simply asking in a normal voice for help in finding a job; he and his family had nothing left and were desperate. After a few minutes he went out, walked straight to the Rossi mills and spoke to the foreman, who agreed to take him on. Soon a queue had formed. Although the winter was hardly over, and there was still snow and ice on the ground, a long line of men, women and children waited patiently outside for their turn to come in and walk, slowly, round the room in which the coffin lay. Some of them surreptitiously cut off pieces of her habit or locks of her hair to keep as relics.

Others pressed into her hands personal belongings - wristwatches, fountain pens, necklaces and wedding rings - leaving them there for a few moments, then taking them back to be treasured always. Women lifted her hands and placed them on their children's heads in blessing. None of the children were frightened, because Black Mother didn't seem at all like a dead person: she hadn't gone stiff or cold, but just lay there smiling and peaceful as if she was only asleep. Late on the Monday afternoon the Sisters were about to close the coffin when a telephone call came from the Rossi mills asking them to wait a bit, as a large number of workmen wanted to come along once the factory closed. The funeral took place on the Tuesday, and after the service at the parish church a procession nearly a mile long wound its way to the cemetery.

Canonisation

Pope Pius X was canonised in 1954. Maddalena di Canossa, who had been beatified during Bakhita's own lifetime in 1941, was canonised in 1988. In the 1960s a Russian Verona Sister, posted temporarily to El Obeid to put some finishing touches to the large mural painting of Our Lady of Africa behind the altar in the Catholic cathedral, had felt inspired to add two kneeling figures in the foreground: Daniele Comboni and Josephine Bakhita, jointly interceding for Sudan. Thirty years on, both were officially beatified by the Pope: Bakhita in 1992, and Comboni in 1996. During the millennium year 2000 Josephine Bakhita was canonised.

During the Mass on that occasion, Pope John Paul II drew out the meaning of Josephine's amazing life in the following words:

"'The law of the Lord is perfect, …it gives wisdom to the simple.'" (*Ps* 19:8)

"These words from today's Responsorial Psalm resound powerfully in the life of Sr Josephine Bakhita. Abducted and sold into slavery at the tender age of seven, she suffered much at the hands of cruel masters. But she came to understand the profound truth that God, and not man, is the true Master of every human being, of every human life.

This experience became a source of great wisdom for this humble daughter of Africa.

In today's world, countless women continue to be victimised, even in developed modern societies. In St Josephine Bakhita we find a shining advocate of genuine emancipation. The history of her life inspires not passive acceptance but the firm resolve to work effectively to free girls and women from oppression and violence, and to return them to their dignity in the full exercise of their rights."

Sources

Dagnino, Maria Luisa, 'Bakhita Tells Her Story', Canossiane Figlie della Carità (Rome, 1993)

Zanini, Roberto Italo, *Bakhita - Inchiesta su una santa per il 2000* (Edizioni San Paolo, 2000)

McEwan, Dorothea, *A Catholic Sudan: Dream, Mission, Reality* (Rome, 1987)

Wheeler, A. (ed.), *Announcing the Light: Sudanese Witnesses to the Gospel* (Paulines Publications Africa, 1998)

Romanato, Gianpaolo, *Daniele Comboni - L'Africa degli esploratori e dei missionari*, (Rusconi, 1998)

Holt, P. M., and Daly, M. W., *A History of the Sudan* (Pearson Education Ltd, 2000)

Werner, R., Anderson, W., and Wheeler, A., *Day of Devastation Day of Contentment* (Paulines Publications Africa, 2000)

Stafford, David, *Endgame* (Little, Brown, 2007)